The **Essential** Buyer's Guide

BMW
Z3
1996-2002

Your marque expert:
Mike Fishwick

T0386712

VELOCE PUBLISHING
THE PUBLISHER OF FINE AUTOMOTIVE BOOKS

First published in May 2017 by Veloce Publishing Limited, Veloce House, Parkway Farm Business Park, Middle Farm Way, Poundbury, Dorchester, Dorset, DT1 3AR, England.
Fax 01305 250479/e-mail info@veloce.co.uk/web www.veloce.co.uk or www.velocebooks.com.

ISBN: 978-1-845842-90-1 UPC: 6-36847-04290-5
Readers with ideas for automotive books, or books on other transport or related hobby subjects, are invited to write to the editorial director of Veloce Publishing at the above address.
British Library Cataloguing in Publication Data – A catalogue record for this book is available from the British Library.
Typesetting, design and page make-up all by Veloce Publishing Ltd on Apple Mac. Printed by Imprint Digital Ltd (UK).

Introduction
– the purpose of this book

Background

At its introduction to the public in the 1995 James Bond film *Goldeneye*, the BMW Z3 was the first mass-market sports car ever made by BMW, and also the first to be manufactured in its new factory at Spartanburg, South Carolina.

The Z3 was developed in Germany over three years by a team led by Dr Burkhard Goschel, mainly using components of the E36 Compact, which, in order to save space, had used the semi-trailing arm rear suspension from the E30 saloon. This was ideal for a small sports car with short suspension travel and high roll stiffness, so reducing the wheel camber change as the suspension operated.

Z3 in the mountains.

The curvaceous body was styled by Joji Nagashima of the BMW California design studio, and, after twenty years, still looks fresh and timeless. The styling was subject to a 'face-lift' in 2000, mainly in terms of the rear wings, which was not universally acclaimed, although these now feature on the majority of the Z3 population and so are accepted as the norm.

The Z3 is officially known as the E36/7, the E36 code ('Entwicklung' or 'development' in German) denoting that the Z3 is a development of the E36 saloon family, which provided most of the engine, transmission, and suspension components, although a certain number of E46 parts were also introduced on later models. This means, of course, that experience, information, and spare parts are readily available at sensible cost, and that the Z3 is well built, rather than being a fragile car with an over-stressed engine and unpredictable handling.

The rare 2.8- and 3-litre Z3 Coupé is not specifically covered by this book, but it obviously shares most of its components with the Roadster. Codenamed E36/8, the Coupé began life as an unofficial project amongst a small group of BMW engineers in Münich, before being adopted for production in LHD form only.

Road tests

The Americans loved the Z3, even in its original 1.8-litre form, but the European motoring writers dismissed

2.8-litre rear – note wider rear wings and wheels.

Early 2.8-litre showing its lines.

it as being "underpowered" – a label which was afterwards applied to all variants – except the mighty M Roadster, which was vaguely dismissed for a "lack of class."

It did not, however, find approval in the motoring press, who, after enthusing about the identical rear suspension of the E30 M3, now found it old-fashioned. *Car* magazine described the Z3 as having "the lacklustre mechanicals of the Compact, clothed in an odd, fish-shaped body!"

When reading contemporary UK road tests one must realise that the average writer passed off their prejudices, gut feelings and mistakes as being facts.

This was usually coupled with an agenda to criticise any product of BMW, which was seen as a builder of saloons for the nouveau riche and was considered an upstart newcomer in the field of small sports cars. It was, therefore, inevitable that the Z3 acquired a reputation as a so-called 'boulevard sports car' which lacked the qualities necessary to provide 'driver involvement' and 'satisfaction.'

It must be realised that any car which cannot perform lurid – even if uncontrollable – power slides will be dismissed in this manner, even if its predictable, safe handling is a far larger bonus. Do not believe all you read!

Prices

Pricing was based upon predicted total sales of 100,000 cars, but at the end of production in 2002 almost 300,000 of BMW's small sports car had found homes.

This was in spite of having to sell for a higher price than the MGF, which, at the time, was also a BMW product, and was itself over-expensive due to the price that Rover Group had agreed for the bodyshell. This meant that the Z3 made far more profit than is normally considered possible for such a niche model.

Although these factors forced the Z3 to begin life as a relatively expensive sports car, it has followed the usual depreciation path, and, as of 2017, has not yet begun to reverse this trend, except in the few cases of 'as new' one-owner low mileage examples. Prices of this 'tomorrow's classic' cannot get any lower, so no doubt values will soon increase – buy yours now!

The Z3 makes a good touring car.

Contents

The Essential Buyer's Guide™ currency "●" equals approximately
At the time of publication a BG unit of currency £1.00/US$1.26/Euro1.17. Please adjust to suit current exchange rates.

1 Is it the right car for you?
– marriage guidance

The Z3 is capable of doing whatever the owner desires, with sharp handing, good luggage space, comfort, safety, and varying levels of performance depending on engine size. When one adds the basic high quality, good equipment levels, high reliability, excellent spare parts and service availability, the Z3 is unbeatable.

Z3 remains pretty with roof raised.

General
Engine sizes range from 1.8 to 3 litres, providing from 110 to 230bhp; sufficient performance to match any sensible requirement.
Rust – the curse of the so-called 'classic' era – is not, so far, a problem, the galvanised body withstanding the ravages of even UK winters.

Fuel types
Most engines used in the Z3 develop their maximum rated power on 98 octane fuel, the exception being the M44 1.9-litre, 16-valve engine, which does so on 95 octane, with about 10% more available when using 97 octane. The lowest permissible octane rating is 91, so they will, therefore, use any fuel available in the civilised world. Unleaded fuel is mandatory, and the engines will operate on fuel containing 5% ethanol. Avoid the 10% ethanol fuel currently being introduced, although BMW states that it is "acceptable."

Face-lift interior is usually brighter.

Driver height
The power-operated seats of the Z3 are adjustable for reach, height, and rake, making

it suitable for a wide range of drivers between about 1720-1883mm (72 and 68 inches) and perhaps a little more or less. The steering wheel is not adjustable.

The door mirrors are electrically adjustable, and in some cases, heated.

Instruments and controls
The controls and instruments follow the pattern of all modern BMWs, and are generally well laid out, with the exception of the switches for the front and rear fog lamps, which are hidden below the instruments and take some getting used to. Some models have a trip computer that's fuel consumption readout can be calibrated to within 1mpg.

The steering rack is the highest-geared of the E36 family, and offers a pleasant feel without being over-sensitive. The steering wheel is frankly too large, but – at a price – it is possible to fit a smaller wheel made by the German company RAID.

Operation of the Getrag gearbox used by the smaller-engined cars is very pleasant, but the ZF box of the 2.8- and 3-litre engines is rather heavy, requiring some concentration in the early stages.

The air-conditioning controls are excellent – simple and tactile knobs for the ventilation system, with push buttons for cooling and recirculation. The driver does not need to divert attention from the road, and can easily operate the system by touch.

Comfort
The standard seats are excellent, offering good support without the 'wrap around' of the sports seats, which can be uncomfortable on hot days. Having said this, the sports seats are sought-after items, mainly for their cosmetic value.

The overall driving position is ideal for anyone up to about six feet tall, and makes the Z3 easily capable of travelling 650 miles (1000km) in a day without causing the usual aching knees and back experienced in normal cars.

Interior space
The Z3 cockpit provides comfortable space for two people, with a surprising amount of room for bits and pieces on a long trip.

The space in front of a lowered hood will accommodate two jackets and fleeces, while the mesh wind blocker can hold a

Driver's view of RAID steering wheel.

Boot space is generous.

Hood is waterproof and secure.

towel inside each roll-over bar. Other clothes can be hung behind the seats, while in front of the radiator, the bumper can also accommodate several items.

Boot space
Unless your idea of packing is to use suitcases, the Z3 boot is ample for two people's luggage, and as the spare wheel is stowed underneath, the usable volume is deceptively large. With practice it can hold everything needed for a long camping trip.

Soft top
The folding hood is one of the very best, and there is only one problem with it – a well-known leak at the point where the windscreen frame meets the seal above the window. This is easily cured by sticking a thin piece of rubber on the ends of the seals. Operation in either direction takes about 10 seconds.

Aftermarket hoods are identical to the original, but lack the zip-in rear window; however, if you look after the window it will outlast the canvas.

General use
The Z3 is a really good all-rounder, and is equally at home cruising at 120mph on a German autobahn or plodding through dense UK traffic jams. In neither case will it overheat or run badly, but will simply get on with the task you have set it with unemotional efficiency.

Ride quality on standard or Bilstein/Eibach suspension is firm and compliant, and will not cause any discomfort.

Insurance
As with any sports car the Z3 provides insurers with an excuse to increase the premium – even though most modern diesel hatchbacks will out-accelerate it! For example, the 2.8 is classed as being in Group 16, so it is obviously advantageous to shop around, and in some cases to join the BMW Car Club in order to qualify for a 'Club Member' policy.

Take care if specifying the engine capacity of a face-lifted 1.8-litre model, as it is in fact 1895cc – the same as the 140bhp 1.9-litre model!

Investment potential

With Z3 prices at what must be an all-time low, (at the time of writing) the only way their value can go is up – subject to condition. This makes a good Z3 into one of the best investments, as this is the 'ground floor' for buyers.

Restoration requirements will be limited, as the overall quality is very good, the mechanicals last forever, and rust is virtually unknown.

Plus points

In an age where modern cars – particularly BMWs – have razor-edge styling, the curvaceous shape does not have a family resemblance, and has aged very well.

Although more modern than the established classics, the Z3 is relatively simple, and is not known for rusting, It is cheap to service and easy live with. Performance is very good, with the 2.8- and 3-litre models having outstanding flexibility and in-gear acceleration.

Boot space is ample for two people, fuel consumption is low, and the soft top is excellent. It is practical, reliable, pleasant to drive, cheap to run, well made, and long lasting – what more could we ask?

Minus points

Now that the Z3 is so cheap, we are going to see many cars which have been driven hard and not maintained. Even cars which have been owned by enthusiasts often suffer neglect in terms of the underside and suspension areas, while in winter batteries are usually left to die of neglect and sulphation.

Many people who imagine that they are experts, after watching television programmes and reading magazines, are sure that the Z3 is a terrible car. This means that complete strangers will insult your car – before driving away in their bland little hatchback!

Will a Z3 fit my garage?

By modern standards the Z3 is quite small, measuring 4025mm long by 1692mm (12 feet x 68 inches) across its folding mirrors. Overall weight varies with engine size – a 2.8, for example, weighs 1335kg (1.5 tons).

Alternatives

While other small sports cars of similar age have firm followings, such as the Mazda MX-5, early Audi TT, and MGF, they do not offer the considerable advantages of the Z3. Equipment levels on all Z3 models are also considerably better.

The Z3 is free from severe structural rust problems, has a larger boot (which does not have to accommodate the spare wheel) and has a wider range of engines than the MX-5.

The Z3 does not suffer from the expensive electronic failures of the early TT, or its turbocharger problems.

The Z3 has far better external vision than the MGF, better servicing access, and lacks the Hydragas suspension problems.

In terms of the 'classic' sports cars it is a combination of the virtues found in the MGB, MGC, TR4a, and Austin-Healey 3000, but without their failings. The Z3 is simply the next generation of the classic sports car, and makes the expenditure, heartache, and problems normally associated with such vehicles a fruitless exercise.

2 Cost considerations
– affordable, or a money pit?

Old (L) and new water pumps.

Modified pulley holding tool.

Drivebelt tensioner locking pin.

Over 130,000 miles and 18 years, my 2.8 Z3 has been the cheapest car to run that I have ever owned, requiring about ⬤x500 of necessary parts, including a set of Bilstein dampers! Anyone who has experienced the costs often associated with 'classic' era cars will be pleasantly surprised.

Servicing
The BMW service schedule is based around oil changes, with the odd replacement of sparkplugs and air filter, but the 'sealed for life' gearbox and final drive, the power steering oil, and the battery are simply ignored. Servicing to a higher standard by anyone who is interested is, therefore, not difficult.

Most maintenance work can be carried out on a DIY basis. Work on the brakes, suspension, and electrical systems are within the scope of a competent home mechanic, independent specialist, or local garage – another advantage of the Z3 being built from standard parts.

Some special tools are required for repair work, but most can be easily manufactured in a home workshop. Examples are a tool for holding the fan pulley while the 32mm coupling bolt is unfastened, and a pin for locking the belt tensioners.

Retracting caliper piston.

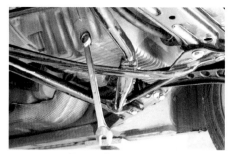
Sump plug removal.

1.9-litre oil filter removal tool.

Oil filter housing is very accessible.

Exhaust cam sensor.

Brake and suspension work requires a simple pressure bleeder, a caliper piston retraction tool, and a spring compressor, all of which are readily available.

Do not worry about the use of a digital engine control unit – regard it as a carburettor and distributor which have fixed settings. Most problems are caused by inlet air leaks, exhaust leaks, worn sparkplugs, and similar. You do not need a computer to perform any routine task, and a fault code reader is necessary only in the last resort – and once the codes have been deciphered they often point to mundane causes which could be found by other means. So-called computer diagnosis simply reduces time in a busy garage by pointing the mechanic in the right direction.

Sets of genuine BMW parts lists, workshop manuals, and wiring diagrams are readily available in CD form at modest prices on internet auction sites, which avoids the usual attempts at secrecy which surround most modern cars.

Tyres

New tyres are probably the most expensive replacements you will need to buy for a Z3, the price dependent on the wheel size. Most models up to 2 litres will be running on 225-50x16s, which are a standard Ford Mondeo-type of tyre. There are a vast range of tyres available in this size, their modest cost making it possible to buy a good brand from ●x200 to ●x300 for a set.

The larger-engined cars – from 2.2 litres, are invariably fitted with seventeen-inch wheels of different rim widths, running on 225-45x17 front and 245-40x17 rear. These tyres are no longer unusual, and provide very neutral handling, but are appreciably more expensive. Expect to pay ●x350 to ●x650 for a set, Michelin and Continental being the most expensive. Falken is a popular mid-range choice at about ⬤x350, with other makes available down from about ⬤x250. Expect about 25,000 miles from a set, the rears usually requiring replacement first.

The spare wheel is a slim 'emergency' type, and works surprisingly well, with little effect on handling. The tyres were made only by Continental, who appear to have lost interest in manufacturing replacements, leaving many owners with a tyre which may be more than twenty years old, making the use of a preventative tyre sealant such as Puncturesafe worth considering.

Branded tyres are available for the Z3 from ⬤x200 per set.

Spare parts

Compared to cars of the 'classic' era, the Z3 is quite modern, and almost all parts remain readily available from both BMW dealers and parts specialists such as GSF, Europarts, etc. Parts not in great demand which are peculiar to the Z3, such as the body sill covers, are usually manufactured in batches, and may, therefore, be subject to late delivery from a BMW dealer.

3-litre silencer.

Normal service parts such as filters and gaskets are of course readily available, as they are standard parts across the model range. Membership of the BMW Car Club will usually qualify for a 10% discount at a dealer, which in the case of a large order may make membership attractive. The use of standard BMW parts also means that spares and service are available across Europe, removing a lot of apprehension from a European tour.

A 'butt strut' makes a big difference to the handling.

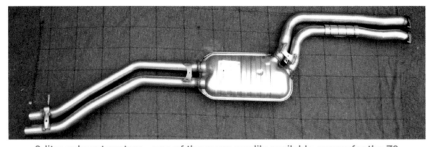

3-litre exhaust system – one of the many readily available spares for the Z3.

The Z3 is basically a modern equivalent to the better 'Classic' sports cars, such as the MGB/C, TR4a and Austin-Healey 3000. Being relatively modern it has a greater dependence on electronics, but to a far lower level than the average modern hatchback. There is nothing to be afraid of.

Handling

The Z3 suspension is based on that of the E36 Compact, derived from the E30 series.

This semi-trailing arm rear suspension is not therefore modern, but in a small sports car with firm suspension, short suspension travel, and a low roll centre it is ideal, and there is virtually nothing to go wrong.

Handling is predictable and neutral, with none of the tail-happy oversteer beloved by the motoring press, unless the driver makes a real effort to provoke

French club driving test.

it – and even then it is difficult. The Z3, therefore, has a greater level of grip than power, providing a high level of safety and the comforting feeling that it will not stab you in the back – even if you make a mistake!

Performance

Performance varies with engine size, although fuel consumption of all models averages about 30-35mpg, which with an 11 gallon (51-litre) fuel tank gives a maximum motorway range of about 300 miles (450km) before the warning lamp operates when 2 gallons (9 litres) remains. In other

1.9-litre twin-cam engine.

words, think about petrol at around 275 miles (400km) and think seriously at 300 miles (500km). On secondary roads these figures can be comfortably exceeded, my 2.8 having covered 220 miles (360km) at an average of 42mpg!

In terms of cruising ability the turbine-like engines are happy at whatever

Some of the camping gear a Z3 can carry.

speed you wish. Maximum speed of a 2.8-litre Z3 is around 135mph, and it reaches it deceptively easily – but remember that such speeds are best used on an empty autobahn.

The engines are all excellent, the popular 1.9-litre, 140bhp engine, for example, provides a far wider range of usable power than the VW 16-valve GTi engine of the same period. The 2.8 will happily pull from 1000rpm in fifth gear.

Acceleration and flexibility are where the Z3 scores over its competitors; a good example being the comparison of the 2.8-litre model with the Porsche Boxster of the period. For example, even *Autocar* (notorious Porsche lovers!) found that when using fifth gear the 2.8 would go from 20-40mph in 8.8 seconds, relative to the Boxster (12.2) with a similar 80-100mph in 9.9 seconds (Boxster 13.4). This means that the Z3 has better 'foot down' performance, and is more relaxing to drive.

Body

Although the boot space is excellent for a small car, a useful increase can be made

Headlamps (masked for Europe).

by removing the CD changer and fitting an MP3 player. Without the CD changer the empty bulge in the forward end of the boot, transforming the amount of usable space.

This allows plenty of soft luggage, tents, folding chairs and table, and all the other items for comfortable camping to be carried. The emergency spare wheel is stowed in a cradle below the boot, so does not reduce boot space.

The folding hood is excellent, being totally waterproof, and taking ten seconds in each direction under manual or power operation.

The panel fit initially appears strange, with 5mm gaps between panels. This is a requirement of US insurers to prevent damage spreading from one panel to the next after a light impact. Virtually all the body panels are bolted to the main structure, making replacement easy.

The doors are quite large, and present no access problems, even for old people with stiff legs, while legroom is of course excellent.

Lights

Headlamp performance is very good, if fitted with modern bulbs such as Philips Blue Vision or Osram equivalents. Avoid all other makes, which generally waste light by scattering it anywhere but on the road. Post-2000 and replacement headlamps are fitted with H7 dip bulbs rather than the HB4 previously used.

Safety

In terms of safety the Z3 is one of the best sports cars, primary roll-over protection being provided by the forged steel windscreen frame, and augmented by the roll-over hoops behind the seats. These hoops were standard fitments on some cars, and can be retrofitted to all but the very earliest models, although a lot of parts are required.

The seat belts are fitted with pre-impact tensioners, operated by pyrotechnic

Spare wheel cradle and Eismann silencer.

cartridges, and the steering column incorporates a collapsible bellows section. One problem area concerns punctures – even if empty the boot cannot accommodate either wheel, BMW supplying a white plastic bag in which the punctured tyre can rest on the passenger's knees. A fatality occurred in which a tyre with an 'egg' in the sidewall was being carried in this manner, a sudden failure expelling air which caused fatal damage to the passenger's lungs. Always fully deflate a tyre before carrying it inside the car.

No problems

The later six-cylinder cars (built from Sept 98) have the double-VANOS engine – meaning automatic timing adjustment of both camshafts – whereas the earlier engines had VANOS on the inlet cam only.

In 2.8 guise they can quickly be identified by the use of small tail pipes with black circular trims – the later engine has larger slightly 'squashed' chromed tailpipes. Unlike the earlier 'M' engines, these engines did not suffer from regular VANOS failures – usually costing about ⬤x2000 per 40,000 miles, or more frequently if you are unlucky!

BMW had a lot of problems with its Nicasil and Galnickel-plated cylinder bores due to the use of high-sulphur fuels, but these engines were never fitted for the US market – which included all Z3 production, where engines with cast iron cylinder liners were always fitted.

Double VANOS engine.

4 Relative values
– which model for you?

As stated, at the time of publication, Z3 values have never been lower, so will inevitably increase. As of 2017 it is possible to buy a good 1997 1.9-litre car for under ●x2000, or a 2002 3-litre model for under ●x4000. In some cases the condition, mileage, and equipment levels may result in a slightly higher price being asked.

Equipment levels
Compared to its contemporaries such as the Boxster, MGF and MX-5, the Z3 was fitted with a wide range of standard equipment which (where available on the other cars) was very expensive. In many cases, adverts now often describe the Z3 standard equipment as if it were optional extras, so it helps, therefore, to know what was standard, and what has been added to the specification.

Z3 wheels come in many styles.

Standard equipment levels on all Z3 models were very good; a typical UK 1.9- or 2-litre model having a driver airbag, traction control, ABS, power steering, limited-slip differential, electric windows, electric seats, electric mirrors, front fog lamps, tonneau, (hood cover) and 16x7 inch alloy wheels carrying 225-50x16 tyres.

The 2.8-litre models were also fitted with roll-over bars, a powered hood, leather seats and door linings, while the 'Sports' version of the 2.2- and 3-litre models had firmer suspension, seventeen-inch BBS cross-spoke alloys and more supportive seats. Dynamic Stability Control was fitted on the 3-litre models, and a passenger airbag was fitted to the later face-lifted models.

Pre-face-lift interior with RAID steering wheel.

Options

Popular options were roll-over bars, a passenger airbag, 17-inch wheels, air-conditioning, cruise control, wind blocker, heated seats and mirrors, and occasionally a hardtop. Many cars were fitted with 17-inch wheels, front rim widths being 7½ inches and rear 8½ inches carrying tyres of 225-45 (front) and 245-40 (rear).

If in doubt, any BMW dealer can use the last seven digits of the VIN code to print out the car's original specification, in terms of standard, standard optional (specified for a particular market area) and optional (customer-specified) equipment.

Obviously, a standard 1.9 will be worth less than a well-specified 1.9, which, in turn, will be worth less than the larger-engined models with similar equipment levels. With prices currently so low, it is difficult to give these differences in terms of percentages, but the difference between cars with such equipment variations is probably around ●x1000. Hardtops and AC Schnitzer wheels are in short supply and high demand, being possibly worth another ●x1000.

Most aftermarket equipment is not worth anything, such as non-standard exhausts, particularly if noisy, although Eisenmann exhausts – of high quality although noisy – are popular. Exceptions are Weismann hardtops, RAID steering wheels, and any AC Schnitzer or Hartge equipment.

Avoid non-BMW alloy wheels, some of which may be replicas of uncertain origin, or fitted using spacers. Be sure that any apparently BBS or AC Schnitzer wheels are genuine, and do not be influenced by their cosmetic value.

The cost of reverting to standard, or at least equipment of known quality, should be remembered when making an offer.

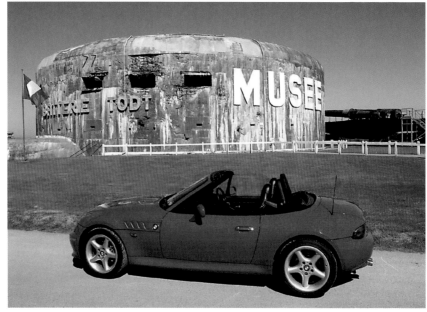

Z3 at the Atlantic Wall – with five-spoke alloy wheels.

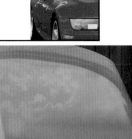

There are few things worse than travelling to view a car which does not live up to your requirements, so it's important to decide on the exact specification you want.

Decide on the engine capacity and the various options you want, then short-list the more desirable models, but do not be in a hurry, for there are still plenty of Z3s around, so you can afford to pick and choose.

Optional equipment

Consider the optional equipment you want – such as a leather interior. This is almost essential, as anyone who has had to sit on a wet fabric seat will confirm! Some models, such as the 2.2, have a leathercloth covering which is almost as good, but lacks the 'breathing' ability of leather.

Air-conditioning in an open car is often derided as being unnecessary, but it has several

Hardtop ready to be stored for summer.

functions. When the roof is lowered on a hot day, it provides a refreshing flow of cool air to ward off heat stroke and aid concentration, and can cool food items when placed below the passenger footwell vent. If the hood has to be raised after the cockpit area has become damp, it will act as a powerful and instant demister, and, while driving in cold weather, will provide demisting without turning the inside of the car into a mobile sauna!

Roll-over bars are another essential, as is a mesh wind blocker, which will eliminate the otherwise powerful back draught. It also reduces headlamp glare from following traffic. A wind blocker will, however, increase the time required to raise the hood, making the optional hydraulic

Pre-face-lift leather interior.

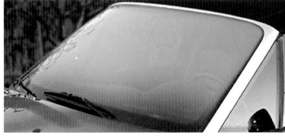

Chrome windscreen surround.

Early 2.8 rear wings.

Face-lift rear wings.

power operation highly desirable.

Wheels are often selected for their cosmetic value, and with so many choices you may find the 'ideal' car has wheels you dislike. Always include any associated cost in your decision, but remember – used BMW wheels of all kinds are readily available, subject to them having the correct offset to suit the Z3, the factory standard being 41mm.

The pre-September 1998 cars had black windscreen frames (simply a layer of adhesive tape, which, with a hair drier and some alcohol, can be removed to reveal the body colour as on the later cars). Cars of all ages may have a chromed windscreen frame, which was an option, secured by use of double-sided tape and being clipped under the rubber seals. It can therefore be retrofitted to any model.

You may find a car with a hardtop, which fits over the stowed hood, and was invariably painted in the same colour as the body. The rear window was electrically heated, the wiring being pre-fitted inside the car. Unless you prefer strict originality, hardtops look far better in gloss black, particularly on light-coloured cars.

Rear wings

All 2.8 models have 2.5 inches more rear track, the pre-2000 models having the wings 'stretched' outwards and downwards across the tyres, generally known as the 'wide body' type.

All post-2000 models use rear wings which are 'humped' on top, and are often also referred to as 'wide body,' but should not be confused with the wings used on the original 2.8 and the M Roadster. With 16x7 inch wheels, they look too wide, but go well with the optional 17x8½ inch rear wheels fitted to the 'Sports' models.

Face-lifted models

Apart from the rear wings, most changes were minor, including chrome rings around the headlamps, an aluminium covering for the centre console, which now carried an analogue clock, outside temperature gauge, and the trip computer in a circular housing. The hood now had a fabric lining (which often comes loose) and the central brake lamp lens was vertical, and mounted on a chrome adaptor.

These brake lamps often leak water into the boot. The reversing lamps were mounted on the boot lid, and the rear crossmember at the back of the boot was larger. The number and quality of spot welds on the boot floor was increased around the area, which has been known to split.

Engine types

The smaller engines are easily identified, the 1.8 being a typical single overhead camshaft design, and the 1.9 a classic double overhead camshaft type.

However, there are three types of six-cylinder engines – the M52 and M52tu (technical update) and the M54. It is therefore important to understand the differences. The M52 was BMW's usual type of twin-cam 24-valve engine, differing from the previous M50 engine by having a single VANOS timing control of the

Single VANOS engine.

DISA control valve.

inlet camshaft, the identification point being the protruding VANOS unit in front of the inlet camshaft. This engine was only fitted to the Z3 in 2.8-litre form.

This engine was revised for the 1999 models (ie manufactured from September 1998) into the M52tu version, fitted in 2- and 2.8-litre form. A 2.5-litre version was sold in the USA, badged as a 2.3-litre, reflecting its lower power when compared to the later 2.5-litre version fitted in the 3 Series, etc.

The M52tu specification included VANOS control of both camshafts, DISA control of the inlet manifold, twin catalytic converters, and a rear silencer which has 'Quiet' and 'Noisy' outlets. A vacuum-operated valve closes off its 'noisy' side below about 2500rpm. These engines produce the same level of power and torque as their predecessors, but the torque curve is flatter, and peaks earlier. Look for the two VANOS units below the front of the cam cover.

The M54 2.2- and 3-litre engines dated from 2001, and were a development of the M52tu, with various detail changes including a 'drive by wire' throttle control. In many cases these engines consume more oil than the older ones, but this is not indicative of any problems, and use of a thicker 5-40 viscosity engine oil can reduce this. They can be identified by the positions of their catalytic converters on the exhaust manifolds, the associated bulging heat shields characteristic of the type.

VANOS and DISA

VANOS uses engine oil pressure, controlled by a solenoid valve, to apply hydraulic pressure against a piston which then forces a second piston, carrying helical splines, through the camshaft sprocket and into the camshaft. This has matching splines, and so rotates slightly, changing the relationship between the sprocket and camshaft, and therefore adjusting the valve timing and power in the mid-range. DISA is an electrically-operated valve which closes a passage in the plenum chamber connecting the throttle body to the inlet pipes, separating the front and rear two groups of three. This has the effect of increasing torque at certain points in the rev range. A six-cylinder DISA manifold can easily be identified by its flat-top and the DISA unit on the side.

The 1.8 and 1.9 four-cylinder engines have a different form of DISA, mounted in a convoluted intake manifold.

Z8 screen washer nozzle.

Where is the car?
Travelling to view a potential purchase is not to be taken lightly, as you may feel under pressure to buy. If you do have to travel, try to view several potential purchases in the same area. Many owners have even travelled to Germany in search of the rare 2.8-litre Z3 Coupé.

Always arrange to view the car at either a dealership or the owner's home – and never in the dark or in a pub car park! If you like the car, make very sure of the ownership status before travelling.

Dealer or private sale?
With Z3 prices now so depressed, they provide little profit for a dealer, so it is highly likely that any car advertised in a specialist dealership is being sold on behalf of its owner. Do not ignore such a car, treat it as you would any other, and ask about its history, equipment, and owners. You are likely to find such a car

Chrome door handle cover.

1.8 manifold and VANOS.

Stainless exhaust and rear suspension.

at a small specialist BMW dealer, tucked between the usual 3 and 5 Series saloons.

A dealer may be more willing than an owner to give you an extended demonstration drive under trade plates, and may offer a warranty, which is an advantage.

Provenance and paperwork

Due to current UK regulations regarding transfer of vehicle ownership, it is now virtually essential to return after arranging the changes and obtaining insurance.

You may wish to place a deposit, purchase being subject to a satisfactory check with HPI, etc, that the car has not been stolen, nor is the subject of an insurance write-off or outstanding credit payment. You may also wish to arrange for a professional inspection by the AA or RAC.

Front RH suspension.

The additional time involved will also give you time to arrange for payment, preferably by a bank cheque, which gives you control until the very last minute.

Make sure that the owner will be selling the car with its Registration Document and a new, or at least current, MoT certificate, which will give you some breathing space after purchase. If the seller cannot produce these documents, or makes weak excuses and promises, forget about the car and walk away.

Rear LH suspension.

Butt strut and body brace.

Strut brace.

Bilstein damper.

Front RH brake disc and caliper.

Conversions and customising

It is always worth asking about modifications, as many may invalidate your insurance policy without making a worthwhile improvement.

Modified BMW engines are not common in the UK, where most owners prefer to add shiny bits of trim.

However, the 2.8 engine will produce an extra 30bhp/30lb-ft when fitted (single VANOS engines) with the intake manifold from the old 2.5-litre engine, or that from the later 3-litre engine for the double VANOS type. This is due to the 2.8 having been purposely limited by a small-bore manifold to fit into BMW's marketing strategy.

As the cars are now quite old, it will not be unusual to find an aftermarket exhaust system – probably noisy – and perhaps some rather tasteless pieces of imitation wood, carbon fibre, or aluminium trim stuck to the centre console, etc. These can usually be removed without damage to the surface underneath – and of course you may come to like them!

One of the few tasteful additions are chrome Z8 washer nozzles, which fit easily, and are of the heated variety.

The BMW 'M' logo attracts many people, and, from 1998, cars were fitted with steering wheels and gear knobs bearing this logo. Some owners also fit side gills and the oval mirrors from the M Roadster.

Suspension modifications

Another popular modification is lowered suspension, often to excess. Basically lowering by more than a 20mm is a sign of the 'slammed to the floor' brigade, who prefer fashion to function, and forget that they are causing the driveshaft constant-velocity joints to articulate beyond their optimum position. Such extreme suspension kits are often sold with poor-quality dampers, and springs which are prone to cracking, so if the rest of the car meets your requirements replace them with either standard of sensibly-modified parts.

Sensible suspension modifications

are systems such as Eibach springs and Bilstein dampers – but I advise owners to retain the standard rear springs, as the Eibach replacements are simply too low when combined with a passenger, full luggage, and a well-cambered road.

Strut braces are quite popular, and usually make a small improvement to initial steering response, but not in proportion to their cost! The better types are straight, joining the suspension struts directly, such as the steel type from Strong-Strut of Scotsdale, Arizona.

For a real improvement it is necessary to fit rear suspension and body bracing struts, also from Strong-Strut. Rubber suspension bushes deteriorate with age, and can usefully be replaced by standard, BMW M types, or polyurethane equivalents. If the car is fitted with seventeen-inch wheels the M or poly bushes are preferable, as – if the rest of the suspension system is in good condition – they will prevent the disconcerting 'tramlining' effect often experienced on poor quality roads. This is caused by the stiffer tyre sidewalls overloading the original bushes at the rear of the front wishbones.

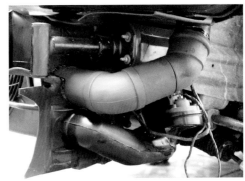
Cold air intake. Note bumper shock absorber.

Probably the best Z3 suspension package is that used on the 2.8-litre coupé, in terms of springs, dampers, anti-roll bars and wishbone bushes. It provides an ideal pattern for suspension modifications.

Brakes
BMW tends to be miserly about its front brakes, the smaller-engined models having solid 288mm discs, the 2.8 having vented dsics of the same size,

Over-modified or stylish? Depends on taste.

and the 3-litre the 300mm discs from the E46 saloon. Many owners have fitted the E46 brakes, which allow the original calipers to be retained, while providing additional braking capacity at reasonable cost.

Air intakes

Another popular modification is a large K&N air filter, or sometimes a Simota-type 'ram air' filter unit. There are many sound technical reasons to discard K&N filters, while the Simota type is merely a K&N filter in a tube, which, when contained in the engine bay, cannot provide any ram-effect whatever, and breathes warm air, so reducing engine output. These are a cosmetic modification, owners admitting that their attraction is the extra intake noise!

A better modification is to arrange a cold air intake, so avoiding the original restricted intake path and feeding the engine with air at ambient temperature. This can easily be manufactured from 70mm rainwater pipe at little cost.

Z4 6-speed gearbox – a worthwhile and popular modification.

Gearboxes

A really worthwhile (and relatively cheap) modification for the 2.8- and 3-litre cars is to replace the gearbox with the 6-speed type found on the 3-litre Z4. This gives a 10% higher top gear with corresponding fuel economy improvement, and a gear for every occasion. It is necessary to shorten the front section of the propeller shaft by 40mm, re-balancing not usually being required.

Remapping and fuel

Remapping the engine ECU is always worthwhile, returning the engine to its optimum settings and giving a small improvement throughout the range, with a proportionally greater gain in the mid-range, and improved fuel economy. Do not expect large power gains; in many cases the improvement is similar to that provided by the use of 97 octane fuel – if you can find it! Fuel is now being adulterated with increasing levels of ethanol, higher-octane fuels simply having a higher level of this cheap alcohol. Remember that alcohol is a good octane booster, but a very poor fuel.

General

If you are looking for a 'tomorrow's classic' you will need a basically original car, which has not had the mixed blessing of an 'enthusiastic' owner. How you view modifications depends on how strong your originality fetish is, in which case you may be happy with the E46 brakes, 3-litre manifold, a non-original hood, and a non-original stainless steel exhaust system. Otherwise, you may want a perfectly original car, even down to the tyres and battery, but may have to be satisfied by gradually fitting original parts. If, however, you want a car to use frequently, you may find that a car with sensible modifications suits your requirements better – it's up to you.

6 Inspection equipment

– these items will really help

Before you rush out the door, gather together a few items that will help as you complete a more thorough inspection:

This book
Reading glasses (if you need them for close work)
Magnet (not powerful, a fridge magnet is ideal)
Torch (flashlight)
Probe (a small screwdriver works very well)
Mirror on a stick/phone on selfie stick
Digital camera/phone camera
A friend, preferably a knowledgeable enthusiast

This book is designed to be your guide at every step, so take it along and use the check boxes to help you assess each area of the car you're interested in.

Don't be afraid to let the seller see you using it.

Take your reading glasses if you need them to read documents and make close up inspections.

A magnet will help you check if the car is full of filler, or has fibreglass panels. Use the magnet to sample bodywork areas all around the car, but be careful not to damage the paintwork.

Expect to find a little filler here and there, but not whole panels. There's nothing wrong with fibreglass panels, but a purist might want the car to be as original as possible.

A torch with fresh batteries will be useful for peering into the wheelarches and under the car.

A small screwdriver can be used – with care – as a probe, particularly in the wheelarches and on the underside.

With this you should be able to check an area of severe corrosion, but be careful – if it's really bad the screwdriver might go right through the metal!

Be prepared to get dirty. Take along a pair of overalls if you have them. Fixing a mirror at an angle on the end of a stick may seem odd, but you'll probably need it to check the condition of the underside of the car. It will also help you to peer into some of the important crevices.

You can also use it, together with the torch, along the underside of the sills and on the floor. A selfie stick and mobile phone can perform the same function.

If you have a digital camera, or your mobile phone has a good camera, take it along so that, later, you can study some areas of the car more closely.

Take a picture of any part of the car that causes you concern, and seek a friend's opinion.

Ideally, have a friend or knowledgeable enthusiast accompany you: a second opinion is always valuable.

www.velocebooks.com / www.veloce.co.uk
Details of all current books • New book news • Special offers • Gift vouchers • Forum

28

– walk away or stay?

It is said that 'You get what you pay for' – and this is no more true than in the used car market. You should, therefore, be sure that you are happy with every aspect of your car, relative to the price paid.

Due to its galvanised body, rust is not a problem, with only a few cars even showing problems with the detachable body sill covers. This means that due to its relatively low age, major problems should not apply to a Z3 purchase.

The owner

Some apparently immaculate cars are a mass of corrosion underneath! Look at the underside, which will give a picture of the amount of care the car has experienced and, if possible, get an impression of the owner and their usage, and avoid the 'dump the clutch at 5000rpm' brigade! Likewise, a low-mileage car should be suspected of having covered many short and cold runs, which, when combined with an occasional oil change, is a recipe for internal engine corrosion. While the engines are virtually bullet-proof, such usage amounts to deliberate cruelty!

Ask the owner how long they have owned the car, and why it is being sold. Avoid cars which have been owned for a short period, or are being sold due to a 'lack of power,' pointing to the car having had a short but hectic life. Ideally, look for a car which has had a mature owner for many years, and a history of long journeys coupled with sensible use.

Certification

Open the bonnet and ensure the VIN code shown on the Registration Document matches with the one stamped on the data plate and also shown in the lower LH corner of the windscreen. Check the registration number and VIN with those on the on the MoT or SORN certificates.

Most Z3s will have some evidence of expenditure on servicing by a BMW dealer or an independent specialist, and some enthusiasts advise never to buy a car without a full service history by a BMW dealership. Although many people regard such paperwork as the Holy Grail, they are nothing more than a collection of rubber stamps, signifying expensive oil changes!

Body condition

A good initial guide to the condition of any car is to kneel in front of it, about a metre from the sides, with your eyes at headlamp level. Move your head to see if there

1.8 and 1.9 front apron.

2.8 apron – face-lift models are similar.

are any ripples on the sides, which are indicative of dents and poor repairs. Use a magnet to check for the presence of filler. The doors are not fitted with rubbing strips, so are particularly prone to damage from careless parkers, who seem to think nothing of opening their doors against another car.

Use the same technique on the bonnet (which is an expensive replacement) and run your hands over all body panel joints to check for accurate alignment. The rear of the bonnet is particularly prone to damage if an attempt has been made to close it with the gas struts mounted in their 'service' position. In such a case the rear sides of the bonnet will have stretched slightly outwards.

Early 2.8 rear wings.

Check the paint on the lower parts of the doors, rear wings, and body sills for bubbling; a sign of rust. This is unusual, but do not allow the galvanised body to make you complacent.

All gaps between panels should have an even 5mm gap – if in doubt use the blunt end of a 5mm drill bit as a guide – but expect a variation between the front apron and the lower front edges of the bonnet. Being plastic, the apron is difficult to align accurately, a poor fit often being a sign that it has been removed for repainting.

Face-lift rear wings.

Check that the doors, boot and bonnet open and close easily, and also that they lock securely, using both the key and central locking.

Try to gently rotate the door mirrors, but do not force them if they do not move, as their pivots are often corroded to the point of seizure or even fracture. Periodic lubrication would save a lot of money, as good used mirrors are very difficult to find. Check their current price before viewing, as this would be an expensive defect.

Do not worry about light misting inside the headlamp covers, as this will usually be 'breathed' out as the headlamp warms up.

Paint

Paintwork quality is generally good, even with metallic paints, but that on the front and rear plastic aprons and mirrors quickly fades, resembling a bad colour match. The reason for this is that these components were not coated in a good plastic primer before painting.

You may be surprised to find an apparently different colour of paint in the non-visible areas, such as the engine bay, boot, under the bonnet, and the boot lid. This paint will be matte rather than glossy, and is a BMW peculiarity, no lacquer being applied in these areas. Likewise, you may find some fasteners, such as on earthing points, which are also painted, the nuts being fitted before painting to protect the threads of their studs.

Boot

Open the boot lid, lift out the carpet, and check the forward area of the floor for cracking and pulled spot welds: a sign of the clutch being regularly dropped to produce maximum acceleration, by an unsympathetic owner. In such cases there will doubtless be further damage underneath, centred around the final drive torque stay. Rectification, while possible, is expensive, and in such cases you should walk away.

While the boot is open check the wiring between the body and boot lid, as the sheathing often splits, and can also break up inside the sheathing, preventing the driver's door central locking from operating. Repair is straightforward; a repair kit is available from BMW.

Look for amateur wiring around the battery and at the LH side of the boot, where a large stereo amplifier may have been fitted. Check the battery voltage with the engine stopped and running, and look for corrosion around the battery well.

Again, look for signs of amateur wiring, particularly if HID headlamps have been fitted. These lights seldom meet UK standards, even if an MoT has been passed, and only improve the dipped beam. Ask for the original headlamps, as new ones are around ●x400 a pair.

Under the bonnet

Check the radiator core and around the cylinder head for any sign of coolant leaks (the 1.9-litre 16-valve engine is prone to leak from the head gasket and header tank) and from all hose joints.

Look at all the flexible coolant hoses, checking for leaks and damage, and also press your fingers around the large ribbed rubber elbows between the airflow sensor and throttle body feeling for damage. Check the hose at the front RH corner of the cylinder head, between the secondary air pump and the air control valve. This is fitted on most pre-2000 cars, to reduce emissions after start-up, and failure of the valve diaphragm can pass hot exhaust gases into the rubber pipe, melting it. This is not a problem, as the air pump is required for the US market only, and can be removed, along with its control valve. BMW dealers can supply a steel plate to blank off the hole.

Double VANOS engine.

Check the paint code on its label at the front of the LH strut tower, and be sure it is the colour you want – particularly if viewing in poor light. Also check the year and month of manufacture, on the label at the front of the RH strut tower.

If buying a late 1998 2.8-litre model, check to see if the engine has single or double VANOS operation. Double VANOS was introduced after the factory shutdown, during September 1998, and can make a difference to the price. It is possible that an earlier car was sold during autumn 1998, so be sure that the engine is what you are expecting to see.

Check the condition of the tonneau cover, a hood cover which is pretty, but a nuisance to use – particularly when it is raining.

Remove the oil filler cap and look for rust or creamy deposits of emulsified oil, which is usually a sign of excessive cold running, but could be due to a leaking head gasket. Oil leaks from the cam cover are often a sign that the crankcase breather cyclone trap needs to be replaced, an inexpensive and easy task.

Check the engine oil level, which should be in

Antifreeze hydrometer in use.

the upper half of the 'min' to 'max' range. Wipe a little onto your fingers and smell it – it may smell of petrol, a sign of excessive cold running and the need for an oil change.

Also check the coolant level, and use a hydrometer to check the antifreeze proportion. Should this be about zero, it may be a sign that the coolant has been replaced by water to mask a coolant leak. In such a case, ask some probing questions.

Interior

Set the seat to a comfortable position, adjust the mirrors to suit and turn on the ignition, checking that the fuel gauge gives a reading. It often sticks at around the half-way mark, due to a faulty level sensor in the fuel tank, which is in unit with the fuel pump. As the car will usually use fuel at 30-35mpg, the trip distance counter is a good guide to refuelling – 275 miles is a decent distance at which to fill up.

Although BMW suggests a new 'Gold film' sensor at ●x150, the use of 97 octane fuel tends to

Face-lift interior.

prevent sticking. Holding a foot on the brake pedal, start the engine, and check that the pedal depresses as the engine starts and vacuum is built up in the servo.

Oil filter parts – note small 'O' rings.

Air con drive belt tensioner.

Make sure that the red low oil pressure warning lamp goes out as soon as the engine starts. If not, it could be a sign that the vital 'O' rings inside the oil filter are damaged or missing, reducing the oil supply to the bearings. This may be accompanied by a rattle, on starting, from the cylinder head, showing that the hydraulic tappets are being starved of oil. In such a case, walk away; with plenty of Z3s around, there is no point in taking a chance.

The orange oil warning lamp may flash a few times after the engine is switched off – this is a low oil level warning, operated by a level sensor after a litre has been used – the difference between 'Max' and 'Min' on the dipstick.

Check that all gears engage smoothly, both before and after starting the engine. If the lower gears are difficult to engage, maintain pressure on the gearlever and stop the engine – if the gear now engages, it is a sign of clutch drag, due to either a worn clutch plate or one which has swollen after absorbing moisture. In either case, a modern replacement will be necessary.

Restart the engine and listen for a continuous rattle from the front end, and, if fitted, engage the air-conditioning compressor and see if any rattle becomes worse. If so, this is a sign that the belt tensioner pulley bearing is badly worn. Replacement is easy – a new pulley costs about ●x30. If the noise remains the same, the auxiliary drivebelt tensioner will probably be the cause – check the tensioner pulley for free play.

Lower frequency rattles or grinding noises from the front cylinder head area signify worn

Fan coupling nut removal.

33

VANOS splines, which is as unusual as it is expensive – in this case, walk away.

Stop the engine and check the engine-driven cooling fan for fore, and-aft, play at the tips of the blades (a sign of wear in the bearing of the viscous coupling) and also look for broken fan blades – a common problem on pre-1998 cars, which can often cause damage to the radiator core. Typical life for the coupling is 70,000 miles.

The temperature gauge should quickly reach its mid point, but not any higher. Failure to warm up signifies a failed thermostat, which is very common on cars made between September 1998 and Easter 2000. A hot engine at idle, which cools at higher speeds, is often a sign of the early plastic water pump impeller slipping on its shaft. Modern replacements use a stainless steel impeller, and last for a long time.

Raise and lower the hood, using the power operation if fitted, and check the condition of the rear window, which may be cloudy and scratched, or even damaged by debris trapped in the rear roof seam.

A new BMW zip-in window costs around ●x200 fitted. Inspect the hood fabric and stitching, particularly on the rear quarters, where the fabric and stitching can become worn when folded. A replacement non-BMW hood will cost about ●x600 fitted. If a roof blanket has not been used, the window may be kinked and scratched: these factors may combine to necessitate replacement of the roof.

By now, you should have a pretty good idea about the car's condition, must decide if you are going to walk away or inspect it more thoroughly.

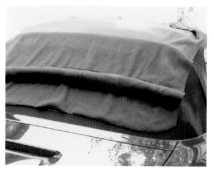
Hood blanket fitted.

Hood blanket in action.

Hood going down.

Note roof blanket position.

8 Key points
– where to look for problems

If you decide to progress you should now have formed a fairly thorough idea about the car, and be ready to consider the more expensive or difficult aspects of purchase. The degree of importance you apply to them depends on whether you are looking for a 'tomorrow's classic' or a 'summer fun' car.

For example, does the car have the correct rear wings? A few cars – mainly 1.9-litre models – have been fitted with 2.8 wide-body or the later 'humped' rear wings, which are appropriate to a year 2000 model.

Expect a humming noise from the pedal area when the ignition key is turned to position 2 – this is the cooling fan to the 'E-box' which contains the engine electronics, and will also run for a short period after the ignition is turned off.

The engine should start easily, but do not let it idle for long. When doing so, expect a strong smell of fuel from the exhaust while cold.

Is the engine quiet and running smoothly? A good engine should be very quiet, free from vibration, and responsive. Are any warning lights operating? A common cause of the 'EML' lamp operating is damage to the rubber inlet elbow between the throttle body and airflow sensor, leaking air and weakening the mixture. The orange oil lamp illuminating when the engine is stopped is a sign that the oil level has fallen to the minimum point. Check this by use of the dipstick.

Are the ABS and/or traction control lights illuminated? This is usually due to the battery being less than fully charged, or occasionally to dirty wheel sensors, and does not necessarily signify impending electronic doom.

The front and rear aprons are mounted on stout aluminium bumpers, which are carried on shock-absorbing struts. If the car has been subject to a light shunt these struts may have been compressed, in which case they do not extend again, making alignment of the apron with the other panels impossible. The effect looks serious, but replacement is not expensive.

About the only area which may be

Check the interior for active warning lights, damaged switchgear and signs of leaks.

rusted are the body sill covers, which are expensive but easy to replace, being bolted on; as are virtually all the Z3 body panels.

Alignment of the window glasses to the rubber seals does not usually give any problems, but is easily adjusted, although setting the vertical limit of window travel is rather more complex. Door and window seal rubbers seem to last forever.

Check the contents of the tool kit, jack, and the presence of the manual, service book, and other publications provided when the car was new. Anything missing can be obtained from a BMW dealership, or purchased secondhand – particularly the tools.

Check the tyres for type, wear, and pressure – BMW tends to recommend rather low pressures, but 2.5 bar (37psi) all round is the optimum. The Z3 is very particular about its tyres, disliking uneven wear and mixed types of tyre.

Lower the spare wheel for inspection – you may find that the owner has never done so, trusting in a mobile phone and

Z3 spare is located under the car's rear. Check carefully, as replacement is tricky.

a credit card. Make sure that the spare has plenty of tread, and is free from cracks between the tread blocks and on the sidewalls. Pressure should be 4 bar/60psi. Remember that a new spare tyre is now unobtainable.

Look very hard at the interior, particularly the carpet, as this cannot be replaced without a major stripdown. Most UK cars were fitted with additional floor mats, so worn carpets are unusual. Check the carpet for moisture, particularly below the doors where water may be let in by a damaged moisture barrier membrane. If in doubt, remove the plastic door sill and feel under the carpet for moisture.

Fabric seats are unusual on UK cars, and, if fitted, may have become worn on their side bolsters, or the weave may have become somewhat 'furry.' In such cases replacement is the best option, ideally by used, leather-covered types.

Raise the carpet behind the storage compartment and check for moisture, as it has been known for leaks to occur at the back of the hood, or around the rear damper mounts if their gaskets have not been replaced. On post-2000 cars check for water in the boot, as the later centre brake lamp is well known for leaking.

Ask to see the latest emissions test figures, and also any previous test figures, as some testers have been known to exaggerate the carbon monoxide levels – understating them is, of course, illegal, but exaggerating them, sometimes by exactly double, is not, and makes for a good business in selling replacement catalytic converters! Another common dodge is to carry out the emissions test on a cold engine – check that the oil temperature is given on the certificate, as anything below 50 degrees means the figure is pessimistic.

By now, you should have decided if this car is for you, and only be interested in looking for serious problems.

9 Serious evaluation
– 60 minutes for years of enjoyment

Circle Excellent (4), Good (3), Average (2) or Poor (1) for each check, and add up points at the end. Any evaluation check must be realistic. Sole responsibility lies with the buyer to be vigilant and not cut corners over the next 60 minutes. Take it seriously, get it right, and you will be able to make an informed decision on whether to purchase. Get it wrong, and it could become your worst nightmare.

Small sports cars are usually bought with the heart rather than the head, but the Z3 is a car which, subject to its limited people-carrying ability, will satisfy the requirements of either. You will now have decided to buy the car, and are looking for serious deal-breakers.

Left-hand drive cars

There are quite a few LHD Z3s in the UK, which have been imported from Europe, including the rare 2.8-litre Coupé. To have been registered in the UK, one can assume that the paperwork is in order, but an enquiry to DVLA is the best way to go.

Make sure that the headlamps have been replaced, by checking that the triangular section of the lens is between the bottom and left hand extremes, as viewed from the front of the car facing backwards. New headlamps cost around ⬤x400 a set.

Security

The Z3 is fitted with a Thatcham Category 1 alarm, locking and immobiliser system; two types having been used, which have different actuating transmitters. Make sure that the system works, and that spare alarm and ignition keys are provided. Some systems have an isolation key for the alarm siren. In the absence of such keys, try to obtain details – serial number, etc – of the system.

Check that the doors and boot can be locked using the key – the locks are often neglected and can be jammed by road grit.

Ensure that the security key for the wheel bolts is present, ideally with a spare key and the code for re-ordering.

The BMW wheel bolts are not difficult to force, the best such security bolts being the McGard polygonal slot type, which should have a spare key. Spare keys are available via its website if you have the serial number.

Wheels

Check for cracking from the securing bolts, and damaged rims due to inaccurate parking. Expect to pay from ⬤x300 for renovation. Cheap after-market wheels are not worth restoring.

The usual range of BMW alloy wheels are well-finished, and should last for up to ten years before corrosion becomes a problem.

The 17-inch BBS cross-spoke wheels used on the 2.2- and 3-litre 'Sports' models, however, soon develop corrosion. These wheels have rims with polished and lacquered edges, which tend to become chipped, so allowing water to spread corrosion beneath the lacquer. The best answer is to have the entire wheel powder-coated in the same colour, but maintaining authenticity demands an original-looking finish to a higher standard. Specialist companies such as Pristine

Alloy Wheels will perform miracles, but at a cost of some ●x300 per wheel.

Make sure that the tyres are of the correct size – some owners have fitted larger-section tyres in an effort to improve the car's 'stance,' but such cosmetic changes contribute nothing, and may affect your insurance. Also check that the speed rating is correct.

Look for the use of wheel spacers, particularly on the smaller-engined cars. This is another cosmetic change, which, in some cases, can overload the wheel bolts and cause misalignment between the hub and wheel.

Body

Do not allow the Z3's galvanised structure to make you complacent – check it as you would on any other car. Run your fingertips along the bottom of the doors, and inside the turned-in edges of the massive bonnet, feeling for roughness which may turn out to be early signs of rust, poor repairs, or just mud. Run your hands in both directions over the joints between all body panels, checking for misalignment. if viewing in less than good light do not be afraid to use a torch to check every panel.

If an attempt has been made to lower the bonnet while the gas struts are in their 'Servicing' position, it is possible for the rear edges to be forced outwards. A new bonnet costs about ●x1000.

Make sure that the bonnet and boot can be held open by their gas struts, and that there are no signs around the edges of having been masked off for a respray.

Boot floor condition

Chock the front wheels and raise the rear end of the car – ideally using two trolley jacks under the rear jacking points, protecting them with pieces of hardwood. Support the centre of the rear

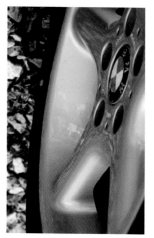

One of the many BMW Z3 wheel styles.

BMW wheel with security bolt and dimensions in centre.

Rear RH suspension.

Stainless steel exhaust.

Detached rear LH ARB link.

Z3 differential (LSD).

CV joint boot.

cross-member with some wooden blocks as a basic safety measure.

Slide under the car, and closely inspect the area of the boot floor from the final drive torque stay and its rubber bush, and along the cross-piece on which it is mounted. This is the area where cracking is known to take place, and while more common on the M Roadster, it is not unknown on the 2.8 and 1.9 models, depending on the number and quality of spot welds and the driver's level of sympathy. Repair is possible but expect to pay about ●x1000, so unless the rest of the car is perfect, and the price allows for it, walk away.

Rear underside 4 3 2 1
Check the condition of the brake hoses and exhaust mounts, and slap the silencers with the flat of your hand and see if they rattle – particularly the front silencer. Does the front silencer rattle when warm, or the rear silencer have lots of rust spots over its body? If so, a replacement cat-back system will soon be required. The pipes and catalytic converter(s) – there are two on the post-1998 six-cylinder engines – are of stainless steel.

Check that the converters are in place, as some owners remove them in a futile quest for an easy power increase. Remember that current MoT test requires that they be fitted.

Check the rubber bushes of the rear anti-roll bar, and particularly the drop links, which, on pre-2000 cars, can often work off the end of the anti-roll bar. The replacements have 'Boge' moulded into their rubbers.

The fuel tank is supported by thin steel straps lined with foam rubber. Inspect the straps for rusting, which often causes them to fail, and that their foam rubber pads are in place. Their loss can cause a loud knocking noise on rough roads, but is easy and cheap to repair. Many owners glue the new pads to the base of the plastic fuel tank rather than the steel strap, which prevents them coming loose again. Look at the spare wheel, checking for tread depth and signs of cracking on the sidewalls and between the tread blocks. Check the condition of the rubber boots on the driveshaft CV couplings, and for oil leaks from the final drive and dampers.

What is the general condition like? So many apparently good cars require a lot of work to bring the underside back to even a reasonable condition, although this work requires effort and enthusiasm rather than money.

Checking battery condition.

Traction control systems ④ ③ ② ①

Most UK market cars were fitted with a limited-slip differential of the Torsen (TORque SENsing) type. This uses a gear train to apportion load, rather than a locking clutch. Its operation is therefore rapid but progressive, most drivers being unaware of its action.

Original wishbone bush.

This is described in the options list as a 'Sperredifferental 25%.' Unless the road is covered in ice it is very difficult to check the LSD operation, so you will have to trust it unless it is making noises when turning round a sharp corner. In such a case an oil change using the approved 75-140 LSD oil may be all that is required.

Powerflex bush parts.

A Torsen LSD should not make any noises, but as they grow old some play inevitably develops, which will make the odd knocking noise. The same applies to the traction or stability control systems (ASC or DSC) and you will have to take them

Front ARB and 'X' brace.

on trust, as unless the warning lamps refuse to go out after a decent run, there is nothing to look at. DSC uses a lateral accelerometer, which is expensive to replace.

After storage

Has the car been stored for some time? If so, in the UK it should have a SORN certificate – otherwise it will cause problems when you come to change ownership. Ask to see the SORN certificate.

Has the battery been kept on charge, or at least periodically recharged? If not, the battery will be past its best, or even useless. Check its terminals for signs of corrosion, and check its date of manufacture, if possible. Check the tyre pressures and all fluid levels before any test drive,

Front underside

Now raise the front wheels in the same manner as you did the rear, supporting the cross member with wooden blocks. Check the engine and gearbox for leaks – the tapered drain plug of the gearbox is prone to leak if not treated with a good thread sealant, and look carefully at the rear gearbox seal, its rubber mountings, and the rubber coupling behind the gearbox.

Check the front suspension for play in the steering and suspension ball joints – the inner wishbone joint can only be replaced as part of a new wishbone, but is not expensive.

Check the engine for oil leaks, and remember that a leaking sump or timing chest will invariably require removal of the engine, and perhaps also the cylinder head.

Look at the rubber bushes of the front anti-roll bar, and those of the drop links, which should be replaced with polyurethane items.

Check the condition of the flexible pipes from the power steering cooler in

Defective thermostat.

Steering rack and pump.

Thoroughly check the interior.

Shortened gear lever.

front of the radiator, and their steel connections, which have been known to rust.

Also, inspect the steel pipe running across the front of the steering rack, which often rusts through. Expect the cadmium plate of the steering rack, and all fasteners, to be badly corroded by the usual UK salt-laden winter. Serious though it looks, this may be nothing to worry about, as cleaning and painting with Smootherite can soon improve matters.

Look for oil leaks from the flexible pipes on the power steering pump, which often benefit from the use of worm-drive hose clips rather than the original crimped type. This work is a good opportunity to change the PAS fluid.

While making your under body inspection look at the brake calipers and hoses, check the remaining thickness of the pads.

Assess any lip caused by wear on the discs while looking through the alloy wheels. Ignore any rust around the edges of the discs; any light rust on the main braking surface should be worn away by the pads under braking during your test drive. Also check the lower side of the floor for rusting and damage – particularly in the front to mid-wheelbase area, looking at the body sills, front chassis rails, and external pipes on the passenger side.

Cockpit

Take a second look at the cockpit area, which should now be looking more familiar – are there any signs of ill-treatment or neglect? The seat frames do not usually give trouble, and their pimply Oregon leather usually lasts very well. While used seats are not too difficult to find and fit, a damaged dashboard is something to avoid.

A few cars had the optional extended leather, covering the top of the dashboard and sides of the console, which often peels back from the edges. Securing it properly is not a difficult job, and it is a sought-after option. Press the trip reset button to display the mileage readout, and check that it agrees with what's shown on the MoT certificate.

Check the operation of the windows, which should run smoothly between their limits. Sit in the seats and attempt to rock them backwards and forwards – any free play is a sign of worn pivot bushes, which are easy and cheap to replace, but something to be aware of. Check the power operation of each seat – in reach and height adjustment, and make sure that the seat belts extend and retract fully.

On a pre-2000 model make sure that the car is fitted with the optional passenger airbag – look for the 'SRS' logo moulded into the airbag cover.

BMW M-Tech steering wheel.

Driver's airbag removal.

Steering wheel

Steering wheels can vary: from the basic E36 type fitted up to about 1998, the 'M' badged wheel fitted up to 2000, and the later two-stage airbag wheel with silver spokes fitted afterwards. All these wheels are somewhat large, and are sometimes replaced by a smaller RAID type, or one of many types without an airbag – although this will result in an MoT failure, as the MoT test now requires an airbag to be fitted where one was original equipment, irrespective of the car's age.

A good compromise is to have the existing wheel re-covered (in the UK this can be done by Royale Steering Wheels, who will do so to your requirements multi-coloured stitching, etc, and slightly increase the thickness of the rim while doing so).

Console

There are two types of centre console – the pre-2000 type, which is all black plastic, with rectangular switches and trip computer (MFA in BMWspeak). Its successor

is aluminium covered, has larger rounded switches, and a trip computer set in a circular gauge-like mounting. This is complimented by a circular outside temperature gauge and an analogue clock set above the heater controls, all of which are surrounded by chrome rings. Apart from the aesthetics, there is nothing to choose between the different types, both of which mount the radio in a standard DIN-sized housing driving six loudspeakers.

Seats

Common colours for the sides of the console and seats, etc are black, blue, cream, tan, and red, often in a mixture.

In the case of any colour but black – particularly pale colours – check the seats for signs of the base black leather colour showing through. Side bolsters on fabric seats are particularly at risk.

Z3 seats available in mixed colours.

Are the seats of the 'sports' type? Try them, as, whilst sought-after, they are not to everyone's taste.

Fuel gauge

Does the fuel gauge move when the ignition is turned on? This is not unusual, as is a failure to fall back as fuel is used, these problems being worse on cars which have not been used for extended periods, and/or filled with 95 octane fuel, which tends to leave gummy deposits on the level sensor. The official answer is to replace the sensor/fuel pump unit with the later gold-plated type, but a few tanks of 97 octane fuel will usually clean it up.

Glass

Check the windscreen for scratches caused by wiper operation on a gritty screen, and small pock marks caused by the now-common debris on UK motorways.

Replacement screens are not too expensive, and insurance companies will usually pay for replacement, so this represents more of a nuisance than an expense.

By now you will have found any serious defects, and maybe a few small problems. Bearing in mind that no twenty-year old car is ever going to be perfect, a few minor problems are to be expected, but on a car with a value of only around ●x3000 you do not need a lot of expenditure to have doubts about the wisdom of buying it.

Road test

Always drive the car before you buy, and be prepared for the Z3 to be different from a normal small hatchback. Remember that you will be driving someone else's car, and also be very sure that you are covered by either your own or the vendor's insurance policy, and check the level of cover.

To begin with, the Z3 will feel far more solid and responsive, with deceptively

Handling is safe and predictable.

Always have a thorough test drive before buying.

good performance. Do not regard a road test as a performance test – you are looking for problem areas, and may find some which are better encountered at moderate speeds. The engine should reach operating temperature – the centre of the gauge – in about half a mile, unless the thermostat has failed.

Wheelspin

Do not expect the car to spin its rear wheels or produce power slides, as this proves nothing, and it is someone else's car, after all. The TorSen LSD is designed to match torque to available grip, therefore producing a smooth and drama-free driving experience.

Tramlining

Find a straight piece of road with a poor surface, and see if the car

Handbrake shoes – RH.

'tramlines,' pulling suddenly from side to side as it attempts to follow undulations and seams in the road surface, when the steering wheel will also jerk in response. This problem is more prevalent on cars with seventeen-inch wheels, the sidewalls of the 225-45 front tyres being far stiffer, and having less internal damping than those of the 225-50 size used with sixteen-inch wheels. The tyres, therefore, transmit sudden loads into the wishbones, compressing the rubber bushes and producing unwanted steering movements.

Although this can be spectacular, the usual causes are uneven front tyre wear and the use of softened or unsuitable rubber bushes at the rear end of the wishbones. New tyres and polyurethane or M3 bushes will usually effect a cure. While on the rough road, listen for rattles from the rear, which is usually a sign that the rear damper top mounts need replacing.

On a smooth road, make small steering movements in both directions, looking for any lack of response, this signifying wear in the steering system.

Brakes

When safe to do so, apply the brakes increasingly hard, checking for response, power, and that the car stays in a straight line. At about 30mph (50kph) apply the handbrake, which operates inside small drums in the rear discs. It will not stop the car rapidly, but its action should be noticeable.

Windscreen wipers

Like all BMWs, the wipers will automatically switch from their lower speed to intermittent operation when the car comes to a standstill. Check for paint damage on the rear edge of the bonnet caused by attempts to replace the wiper blades without moving the arms to their mid position.

Gearbox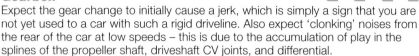

Expect the gear change to initially cause a jerk, which is simply a sign that you are not yet used to a car with such a rigid driveline. Also expect 'clonking' noises from the rear of the car at low speeds – this is due to the accumulation of play in the splines of the propeller shaft, driveshaft CV joints, and differential.

The Z3 demands a very smooth gear change technique, which comes with practice. Change up and down through the gears, lifting off to check for jumping out of gear on the over-run. Expect the ZF gearbox of the 2.8- and 3-litre cars to feel heavy but precise, perhaps with a tendency to baulk when engaging the lower gears at rest – usually a sign of clutch drag, sometimes due to the slave cylinder being in need of bleeding. During low speed changes, check that the engine speed does not rise, this being the sign of a failed clutch switch, a modification kit being available from BMW at modest cost.

If the car has an automatic gearbox, make sure that it runs through all its gears, that the low gear hold function operates, and that the gear change is smooth and positive. An oil change can work wonders for most automatic boxes.

Higher speeds

On a suitable road, run the engine to high speed through the gears, looking for misfiring, clutch slip, exhaust smoke, and any unwelcome noises.

Expect clean and rapid gear changes, with a general lack of drama, but a definite additional urge at about 2500rpm as the VANOS system operates to advance the camshaft timing. If this does not take place, the VANOS seals are probably in need of replacement, 70,000 miles being a typical life before they begin to leak.

Replacement is not a difficult task, seal kits of improved material being available from beisansystems.com.

If you are happy with the car, and have not found any expensive problems, it should be safe to proceed with the purchase.

Evaluation procedure

Z3 in fast company.

Add up the points scored!
88 points = excellent, possibly concours
66 points = good to very good
44 points = average
22 points = poor
Cars scoring over 62 will be completely usable and will require only maintenance and care to preserve condition. Cars scoring between 22 and 45 will require some serious work (at much the same cost regardless of score). Cars scoring between 46 and 61 will require very careful assessment of the necessary repair/restoration costs in order to arrive at a realistic value.

10 Auctions

– sold! Another way to buy your dream

Auction pros & cons

Pros: Prices will often be lower than those of dealers or private sellers, and you might grab a real bargain on the day. Auctioneers have usually established clear title with the seller. At the venue, you can usually examine documentation relating to the vehicle.

Cons: You have to rely on a sketchy catalogue description of condition and history. The opportunity to inspect is limited, and you cannot drive the car. Auction cars are often a little below par and may require some work. It's easy to overbid. There will usually be a buyer's premium to pay in addition to the auction hammer price.

Which auction?

Auctions by established auctioneers are advertised in car magazines and on the auction houses' websites. A catalogue, or a simple printed list of the lots for auctions might only be available a day or two ahead, though often lots are listed and pictured on auctioneers' websites much earlier. Contact the auction company to ask if previous auction selling prices are available, as this is useful information (details of past sales are often available on websites).

Catalogue, entry fee and payment details

When you purchase the catalogue of the vehicles in the auction, it often acts as a ticket allowing two people to attend the viewing days and the auction. Catalogue details tend to be comparatively brief, but will include information such as 'one owner from new, low mileage, full service history,' etc. It will usually show a guide price to give you some idea of what to expect to pay, and will tell you what is charged as a 'Buyer's premium.' The catalogue will also contain details of acceptable forms of payment. At the fall of the hammer, an immediate deposit is usually required, the balance payable within 24 hours. If the plan is to pay by cash, there may be a cash limit. Some auctions will accept payment by debit card. Sometimes credit or charge cards are acceptable, but will often incur an extra charge. A bank draft or bank transfer will have to be arranged in advance with your own bank, as well as with the auction house. No car will be released before *all* payments are cleared. If delays occur in payment transfers, then storage costs can accrue.

Buyer's premium

A buyer's premium will be added to the hammer price: *don't* forget this in your calculations. It is not usual for there to be a further state tax or local tax on the purchase price and/or on the buyer's premium.

Viewing

In some instances it's possible to view on the day, or days before, as well as in the hours prior to, the auction. There are auction officials available who are willing to help out by opening engine and luggage compartments and to allow you to inspect the interior. While the officials may start the engine for you, a test drive is out of the question. Crawling under and around the car as much as you want is permitted, but you can't suggest that the car you are interested in be jacked up, or attempt to do the job yourself. You can also ask to see any documentation available.

11 Paperwork
– correct documentation is essential!

The paper trail

Classic, collector and prestige cars usually come with a large portfolio of paperwork, accumulated and passed on by a succession of proud owners. This documentation represents the real history of the car, and from it can be deduced the level of care the car has received, how much it's been used, which specialists have worked on it, and the dates of major repairs and restorations. All of this information will be priceless to you as the new owner, so be very wary of cars with little paperwork to support their claimed history.

Registration documents

All countries/states have some form of registration for private vehicles, whether its like the American 'pink slip' system or the British 'log book' system.

It is essential to check that the registration document is genuine, that it relates to the car in question, and that all the vehicle's details are correctly recorded, including chassis/VIN and engine numbers (if these are shown). If you are buying from the previous owner, his or her name and address will be recorded in the document: this will not be the case if you are buying from a dealer.

In the UK, the current (Euro-aligned) registration document is named 'V5C,' and is printed in coloured sections of blue, green and pink. The blue section relates to the car specification, the green section has details of the new owner, and the pink section is sent to the DVLA, in the UK, when the car is sold. A small section in yellow deals with selling the car within the motor trade.

In the UK, the DVLA will provide details of earlier keepers of the vehicle, upon payment of a small fee, and much can be learned in this way.

If the car has a foreign registration, there may be expensive and time-consuming formalities to complete. Do you really want the hassle?

Roadworthiness certificate

Most country/state administrations require that vehicles are regularly tested to prove that they are safe to use on the public highway and do not produce excessive emissions. In the UK, that test (the 'MoT') is carried out at approved testing stations, for a fee. In the USA, the requirement varies, but most states insist on an emissions test every two years as a minimum, while the police are charged with pulling over unsafe-looking vehicles.

In the UK, the test is required on an annual basis once a vehicle becomes three years old. Of particular relevance for older cars is that the certificate issued includes the mileage reading recorded at the test date and, therefore, becomes an independent record of that car's history. Ask the seller if previous certificates are available. Without an MoT, the vehicle should be trailered to its new home, unless you insist that a valid MoT is part of the deal. (Not such a bad idea, this, as at least you will know the car was roadworthy on the day it was tested – and you don't need to wait for the old certificate to expire before having the test done.)

Road licence

The administration of every country/state charges some kind of tax for the use of

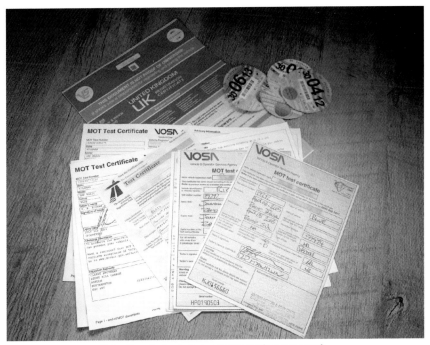

Take time to look through the car's paperwork.

its road system, the actual form of the 'road licence' and, how it is displayed, varying enormously country to country and state to state.

Changed legislation in the UK means that the seller of a car must surrender any existing road fund licence, and it is the responsibility of the new owner to re-tax the vehicle at the time of purchase and before the car can be driven on the road. It's therefore vital to see the Vehicle Registration Certificate (V5C) at the time of purchase, and to have access to the New Keeper Supplement (V5C/2), allowing the buyer to obtain road tax immediately.

If the car is untaxed because it has not been used for a period of time, the owner has to inform the licensing authorities, otherwise the vehicle's date-related registration number will be lost and there will be a painful amount of paperwork to get it re-registered.

Whatever the form of the 'road licence,' it must relate to the vehicle carrying it and must be present and valid if the car is to be driven on the public highway legally. The value of the license will depend on the length of time it will continue to be valid.

In the UK, if a car is untaxed because it has not been used for a period of time, the owner has to inform the licensing authorities, otherwise the vehicle's date-related registration number will be lost and there will be a painful amount of paperwork to get it re-registered. Also, in the UK, vehicles more than 40 years old qualify for free road fund licence – you must still apply in the normal way, but the cost is zero. Car clubs can often provide formal proof that a particular car qualifies for this valuable concession.

Certificates of authenticity

For many makes of collectible car, it is possible to get a certificate proving the age and authenticity (eg engine and chassis numbers, paint colour and trim) of a particular vehicle, these are sometimes called 'Heritage Certificates' and, if the car comes with one of these, it is a definite bonus. If you want to obtain one, the relevant owners' club is the best starting point.

If the car has been used in European classic car rallies, it may have a FIVA (Federation Internationale des Vehicules Anciens) certificate. The so-called 'FIVA Passport,' or 'FIVA Vehicle Identity Card,' enables organisers and participants to recognise whether or not a particular vehicle is suitable for individual events. If you want to obtain such a certificate go to www.fbhvc.co.uk or www.fiva.org; there will be similar organisations in other countries, too

Valuation certificate

Hopefully, the vendor will have a recent valuation certificate, or letter signed by a recognised expert stating how much he, or she, believes the particular car to be worth (such documents, together with photos, are usually needed to get 'agreed value' insurance). Generally such documents should act only as confirmation of your own assessment of the car, rather than a guarantee of value, as the expert has probably not seen the car in the flesh. The easiest way to find out how to obtain a formal valuation is to contact the owners' club.

Service history

Often these cars will have been serviced at home by enthusiastic (and hopefully capable) owners for a good number of years. Nevertheless, try to obtain as much service history and other paperwork pertaining to the car as you can. Naturally, dealer stamps, or specialist garage receipts score most points in the value stakes. However, anything helps in the great authenticity game, items like the original bill of sale, handbook, parts invoices and repair bills, adding to the story and the character of the car. Even a brochure correct to the year of the car's manufacture is a useful document, and something that you could well have to search hard to locate in future years. If the seller claims that the car has been restored, then expect receipts and other evidence from a specialist restorer.

If the seller claims to have carried out regular servicing, ask what work was completed, when, and seek some evidence of it being carried out. Your assessment of the car's overall condition should tell you whether the seller's claims are genuine.

Restoration photographs

If the seller tells you that the car has been restored, then expect to be shown a series of photographs taken while the restoration was under way. Pictures taken at various stages, and from various angles, should help you gauge the thoroughness of the work. If you buy the car, ask if you can have all the photographs, as they form an important part of the vehicle's history. It's surprising how many sellers are happy to part with their car and accept your cash, but want to hang on to their photographs! In the latter event, you may be able to persuade the vendor to get a set of copies made.

12 What's it worth?
– let your head rule your heart

The value of any old car (the Z3 can range between 14 to 20 years old – which is positively ancient by current standards) depends on what one is willing to pay, which, in turn, depends on one's reason for buying.

For any purchase, condition is all-important, which, when combined with the engine capacity and any really useful options, will be the most important factors. At least the Z3 does not yet suffer from the rust problems which can affect some of its contemporaries.

You may want a small sports car as a summer runabout, to be used with the bare minimum of repair work and associated expense; if this is the case, you will be looking for a car which is basically sound, which will spare you any major expense. For example, it should have a new MoT certificate, good tyres, a leak-free hood, and be in generally good mechanical condition with reasonable paintwork and interior. Therefore it should be as cheap as possible, in order to minimise any loss, and perhaps, even yield a small profit.

With this in mind you would be well advised to consider cars fitted with the 140bhp 1.9-litre engine, which is a good performer generally. Such cars can be found for a price of between ●x1000 and ●x2000, depending on condition and specification, although it must be recognised that at such prices, one cannot expect perfection.

Alternatively, you may be looking for a car to keep for some time, which will be a good basis to work on, requiring light restoration work, such as brake and suspension overhauls, a new hood, and, perhaps, some paintwork repairs. In this case, you will be more particular about engine size and type, wheel size and equipment levels. This will usually be an older model, such as a 2.8-litre model from the late 1990s, which can currently be found from ●x2000 to ●x3000, depending on condition.

The later models – with the 2-, 2.2- and 3-litre engines – tend to be bought by people looking for a newer car, which will require a minimum amount of effort and expense to remain in as-new condition for many years. These models retain the highest values, and are all equally popular.

Prices tend to range from ●x2000 for an average 2-litre model to ●x3000 for a equivalent 2.2 or ●x3500 for a 3-litre – with the odd, immaculate, low-mileage example offered for ●x4000. In the case of all these later cars, condition and equipment levels are all-important. The 'sport' variations of the 2.2- and 3-litre models generally attract a premium of ●x500 or so, but it must be remembered that their only real difference is the M Sport suspension, which may be ready for replacement.

In the case of the 2-litre 'baby six', remember that the older 16-valve 1.9 has equivalent performance and handles better, due to the absence of an extra 50lbs of engine weight in front of the axle line. In general, a 1.9 will be preferable to a 2-litre of equivalent condition, particularly as an ex-demonstrator car, as these were very well specified. They can, therefore, be a very good alternative.

The 2.2 model remains a very popular all-rounder, but, if your insurance premium permits, the 2.8 is a better car. Again, it all comes down to condition.

An automatic gearbox is generally held to reduce the car's value, but it may equally appeal to many drivers; they are also very useful for those with certain disabilities, to whom an auto box can be a real asset, and also to drivers looking for something different – an automatic 2.8- or 3-litre model can be very nice.

13 Do you really want to restore?

– it'll take longer and cost more than you think

Restoration in its usual meaning of stripping down, renovating, and rebuilding does not really apply to the Z3, due to its age, freedom from rust, and basic high quality. There are, however, several areas where limited renovation may be necessary, subject to buying the car at a price which allows such activities. There is also one scenario where a large-scale renovation in the normal sense may be necessary.

Limited renovation

This will cover the areas previously discussed, typically repairing normal wear and tear problems in areas such as: tyres, suspension and brakes, minor mechanical replacements, replacing the clutch, hood or windscreen. None of these areas are likely to cost abnormal amounts, and may even represent surprising value.

Medium renovation

Perhaps the most expensive work will be that required to make a good car into an excellent one, in terms of paintwork, hood, windscreen, tyres and exhaust system.

Expect to pay about £2000 for a full respray, £300 for tyres, £600 for a hood, and about £1000 for a new BMW exhaust system, or £500 for a good stainless steel version.

The total costs involved will comfortably exceed the market value of the car, but in the case of a car which will be kept for many years such costs can be ignored, particularly as they can be absorbed over a period of 'rolling restoration' work.

Commitment

In both the above cases, the effort involved cannot compare to that required to bring most older cars up to good condition, which has many advantages, not least that of not being condemned to your garage for the next couple of years!

Large-scale renovation

This really applies to cars which have been accident-damaged and written-off as being uneconomic to repair. Due to the currently low values placed on the Z3 this work may not be as daunting as it initially appears, for light frontal damage is now sufficient to produce an insurance write-off.

With the exception of the windscreen frame and the narrow piece behind the hood, all the visible Z3 body panels are bolted on, which makes replacement a simple DIY project. Even a heavy front impact may not involve the basic structure of the car, as the chassis rails are positioned well back. The bumper is carried on shock-absorbing struts, which collapse to absorb an impact, and bend in response to side loads.

In the case of massive damage the best route is to use a new bodyshell, with a mixture of original, used and new panels. This will not be cheap, but the end result will be a virtually new car, in the colour of your choice.

In this case, do not underestimate the work involved, or the requirement for enough garage space to dismantle the original car and build up the 'new' one.

14 Paint problems
– bad complexion, including dimples, pimples and bubbles

Paint faults generally occur due lack of protection/maintenance, or to poor preparation prior to a respray or touch-up. Some of the following conditions may be present in the car you're looking at:

Orange peel
This appears as an uneven paint surface, similar to the appearance of the skin of an orange. The fault is caused by the failure of atomized paint droplets to flow into each other when they hit the surface. It's sometimes possible to rub out the effect with proprietary paint cutting/rubbing compound, or very fine grades of abrasive paper. A respray may be necessary, in severe cases. Consult a bodywork repairer/paint shop for advice on the particular car.

Orange peel – can be rectified – with work.

Cracking
Severe cases are likely to have been caused by too heavy an application of paint (or filler beneath the paint). Also, insufficient stirring of the paint before application can lead to the components being improperly mixed, and cracking can result. Incompatibility with the paint already on the panel can have a similar effect. To rectify the problem, it is necessary to rub down to a smooth, sound finish, before respraying the problem area.

Cracking – be vigilant when inspecting plastic panels or bumpers.

Crazing
Sometimes the paint takes on a crazed, rather than a cracked, appearance when the problems mentioned under 'Cracking' are present. This problem can also be caused by a reaction between the underlying surface and the paint. Paint removal and respraying the problem area is usually the only solution.

Blistering
Almost always caused by corrosion of the metal beneath the paint. Usually perforation will be found in the metal, and the damage will usually be worse than that suggested by the area of blistering. The metal will have to be repaired before repainting.

Blistering – tends to be localised.

Micro blistering
Usually the result of an economy respray where inadequate heating has allowed moisture to settle on the car before spraying. Consult a paint specialist, but, in most

cases, damaged paint will have to be removed before partial or full respraying. Can also be caused by car covers that don't 'breathe.'

Fading
Some colours, especially reds, are prone to fading, if subjected to strong sunlight for long periods without the benefit of polish protection. Sometimes proprietary paint restorers and/or paint cutting/rubbing compounds will retrieve the situation. Often a respray is the only real solution.

Peeling
Often a problem with metallic paintwork when the sealing lacquer becomes damaged and begins to peel off. Poorly applied paint may also peel. The remedy is to strip and start again!

Dimples
Dimples in the paintwork are caused by the residue of polish (particularly silicone types) not being removed properly before respraying. Paint removal and repainting is the only solution.

Dents
Small dents are usually easily rectifed by the 'Dentmaster,' or equivalent process, that sucks or pushes out the dent (as long as the paint surface is still intact). Companies offering dent removal services usually come to your home: consult your telephone directory.

BMW Z3s have galvanised bodies, and allowing it to fool you into a sense of security could prove expensive! Check the paintwork thoroughly.

15 Problems due to lack of use
– just like their owners, Z3s need exercise!

There are few things that are as bad for a car as lack of use, for this usually means it has been stored in a damp garage and forgotten about.

Think twice about any car which the owner has regularly started up for a short period 'just to see,' as this will produce a lot of moisture inside the engine and exhaust system, which will combine with other combustion products to form acids. These will attack the silencers, timing chains, cam lobes, and other parts.

Neglected? Mouse nest on Z3 intake.

Part-rusted disc – not warped!

Brakes
The car should ideally have been stored in gear, with the handbrake off, as inaction, particularly in damp conditions, can cause the clutch plates, brake pads and discs or handbrake shoes and drums to rust together. This is not as serious as it sounds: to free the clutch, simply start the engine with the brakes fully on, in fifth gear with the clutch disengaged.

To free the brakes, engage first or reverse gear, rev the engine a little, and slowly engage the clutch. The brakes will usually come free with a loud bang.

Do not worry about the coating of rust on the discs, as this will rapidly wear away. Give them plenty of use, and, If in doubt, replace the pads. If the brakes bind, lever the pads outwards against the discs, looking for stiffness that is indicative of the pads having rusted to their carrier bracket. Removal will require some effort, after which a light coat of Copper Slip or similar on the sliding surfaces will restore and maintain normal action.

Battery
So many enthusiasts neglect their battery for months on end, the associated sulphation killing more batteries than anything else. Even an overnight charge will not compensate for the reduced capacity caused by this.

Fluids

Brake fluid absorbs moisture, usually through the rubber hoses. Expect to replace the brake and clutch fluid very soon, bleeding it through the nipples until all the old fluid is purged. The use of a coloured fluid such as the ATE Blue Racing–type provides a useful indicator.

Tyres

If the car has been resting on its tyres, expect some temporary vibration due to the inevitable flat spots this produces. Check the pressures – higher pressures will reduce this effect.

Remember that any tyre over ten years old will have hardened and lost a lot of its grip, particularly in wet conditions.

Rubber and plastic items

Due to the high quality of the rubber-like and plastic materials used by BMW, it will be unusual to find any problems with hoses or window seals, etc, which will usually last the life of the car.

Having said that, it does no harm to slide your fingers over all the cooling system hoses, checking for bulges or oil contamination.

The highly-flexible door seals tend to harden a little, periodic application of WD40 or BMW Gummi-Phledge being wise.

It's worth checking hoses and other plastic/rubberised components.

www.velocebooks.com / www.veloce.co.uk
Details of all current books • New book news • Special offers • Gift vouchers • Forum

16 The Community

– key people, organisations and companies in the Z3 world

Background

BMW has survived a very dramatic history, having been involved in two disastrous wars, five bankruptcies, and two takeovers. Since the 1959 bankruptcy, the company has been controlled by the Quandt family, Doctor Herbert Quandt being considered as its saviour.

BMW is the only car manufacturer to have made a profit every year since 1960. Even so, in the 1980s, it was accepted wisdom that to survive, BMW had to join with a large corporation such as General Motors. It has, however, survived, and become a major player in an industry dominated by giants. Little wonder then, that BMW has attracted such an enthusiastic following.

BMWCC concours.

BMW Z register badge.

Clubs

There are no UK clubs specifically catering for the Z3; the BMW Car Club (GB) Ltd being the only UK car club recognised by BMW. It caters for all models (including the Z3) and areas through its system of type registers and local regions.

It produces a glossy magazine each month, '*Straight Six*,' and organises factory visits, weekends, track days, an annual national festival, and many local events. Most dealers and some specialists, too, offer a discount on goods and services to members.

Membership also gives access to events organised by other clubs within the International Council of BMW Clubs structure. For details, see the club's website: bmwcarclubgb.uk and forum: bmwccgbforum.co.uk

Internet forums

Although there are no other clubs specifically catering for the Z3, there are several BMW forum groups in the UK. They seldom, however, show interest in the Z3, with the exception of: ZRoadster.net and its Z3 forum: www.zroadster.net.

ZRoadster.net has many of the facets one would expect of a club; its members organising events and offering advice on matters from technical to touring subjects. It is the best UK forum for Z3 owners.

There are several racing clubs that sponsor a series for the Z3, using specified suspension and other modifications, aimed at providing cheap and competitive racing – if you are good enough!

European clubs

Although the Z3 was not as popular in Europe as in the UK – there are three major clubs:
France: BMW Z3 Club France: bmwz3club.fr/site/index.php
Germany: Z3 Roadster Club Deutschland: z3-Roadster-club.de
Switzerland: BMW Z3 Club Vierwaldstättersee: bmwz3club.ch/
These clubs organise annual gatherings – the Swiss event in particular being very popular with UK owners.

Specialists

Although there are no dedicated Z3 specialists in the UK, the use of so many E36 and E46 parts means that there are many independent BMW specialists who are able to perform all maintenance and repair tasks at prices well below those of a BMW dealership.

Tuning specialists

Most UK BMW owners are more interested in fitting shiny bits of trim and wider wheels than enhancing their power output, and this applies equally to the Z3.

For this reason it is difficult to find a tuning company of the type found in Germany, where a modified cylinder head and Schrick camshafts can be fitted in a day.

Workshop manuals, etc

The most publicised manual is that by Bentley, but this is expensive and leaves something to be desired, in spite of its impressive thickness. Haynes produces a 3-Series manual of half the thickness and cost, which has sufficient Z3-appropriate content to satisfy most owners.

BMW produces a handy CD set comprising the parts catalogue, wiring diagrams, and workshop manual to cover all models from 1976 onwards, which is a useful addition to a paper manual. These are available from the USA via eBay.

A lot of useful Z3-appropriate information with photographs is included in the 'How to' area of the BMW Car Club forum, covering all the usual tasks which any Z3 owner may have to face.

Useful reference books

BMW Z3 Owner's Handbook – for your car from any dealer (eg: for 1998 models 01.41.9.791.411.En) This contains a lot of useful information in a small book. Downloads in .pdf format are also available on the internet.
BMW Z3 and Z3M Road Tests – Brooklands Books ISBN 1-85520-478-9
BMW Z Series the Complete Story – Mick Walker ISBN 1-86126-424-0

A Z3 is at home in any company.

Z3 club at Rocamadour, France.

Swiss Z3 rally at Interlaken.

17 Vital statistics
– essential data at your fingertips

Model	Number	Remarks
Z3 1.8 Roadster	29,509	8 valve 114bhp non-face-lifted
Z3 1.8 Roadster	17,815	8 valve 114bhp face-lifted
Z3 1.9 Roadster	76,063	16 valve 140bhp non-face-lifted
Z3 1.9 Roadster	1902	8 valve face-lifted
Z3 2.0 Roadster	14,616	face-lifted
Z3 2.2 Roadster	50,147	Includes 2.3 and 2.5 badged US models
Z3 2.8 Roadster	50,607	Includes non-face-lifted & single VANOS
Z3 3.0 Roadster	14,525	
Z3 2.8 Coupé	7671	LHD only
Z3 3.0 Coupé	3853	LHD only

Total production number: 279,273

Performance figures
With so many different engines, space does not permit detailed performance tables for each model, but the 140bhp 1.9-litre and 193bhp 2.8-litre models are a good guide. (Figures from various sources)

Speed	1.9-litre 140bhp	2.8-litre 193bhp	Gear
0-60 (0-100kph)	10.5 secs	6.7 secs	1-3
0-80 (0-130kph)	17.5 secs	11.3 secs	1-3
0-100 (0-160kph)	25.5 secs	18.8 secs	1-4
40-60 (60-100kph)	10.5 secs	8.0 secs	fifth
60-80 (100-130kph)	11.5 secs	8,5 secs	fifth
70-90 (115-145kph)	13.6 secs	8.8 secs	fifth
80-100 (130-160kph)	14.5 secs	9.9 secs	fifth
Max	127mph (200kph)	140mph (220 kph)	fifth

Dimensions
Length – 144in/4025mm. Width – 66in/1692mm. Height – 49in/1288mm.
Turning circle – 34ft /10m. Fuel tank – 51 litres/11imp gall /12.5US gall.
Weight – 1.35t /1335kg. Steering – 2.9 turns lock-to-lock.
Wheels – 7x16 with 225-50 tyres (UK standard) 7½x17 front with 225-45 tyres and
8½x17 with 245-40 rear (optional).

The Essential Buyer's Guide™ series ...